March 14,:

To Ms. Faith White

New Birth Missionary Baptist Church

May the Lord continue to
bless this church!

Joyce Ann Whitlock

Julie The Dreamer

JOYCE ANN WHITLOCK

authorHOUSE®

AuthorHouse™
1663 Liberty Drive
Bloomington, IN 47403
www.authorhouse.com
Phone: 1-800-839-8640

First published by AuthorHouse 2/25/2010

ISBN: 978-1-4490-4231-8 (e)
ISBN: 978-1-4490-4229-5 (sc)
ISBN: 978-1-4490-4230-1 (hc)

Library of Congress Control Number: 2010901803

Printed in the United States of America
Bloomington, Indiana

This book is printed on acid-free paper.

Dedication

This book is dedicated to my beloved mother and father, who taught me how to love and respect my fellow man, and who instilled those basic moral principles that shaped my siblings and me to become productive citizens.

My father sacrificed so much for his family, and made it possible for me to reside in this hallowed place as I write this book. He taught us how to be beautiful inwardly, and gave each of us the genetic gift of exquisite taste in choosing nothing but simple elegance in our dress attire.

My mother, the bedrock and the matriarch of the family, taught us to never settle for anything other than the highest achievement; she stood beside each of her children, coaching and encouraging them regardless of how impossible the task at hand appeared. It was her fortitude, wisdom, vision, and love that helped us to be triumphant in any goal we pursued.

May they rest in peace.

Table of Contents

Chapter I

The Delivery

It was a bitter cold December morning, and Christmas was fast approaching. Margaret was rushing preparing to bake—pound cake, coconut cake, sweet potato pie, and pecan pie—when suddenly she began to experience such severe abdominal pain that it forced her to sit down. She tried to convince herself that if she sat for a while the pain would dissipate, but in reality she was very familiar with this type of pain. These were labor pains. There was no doubt in her mind; after all, she had had four previous pregnancies. She sighed, discouraged; she didn't want to have to stop everything, go to bed, and prepare for an arduous night of deep breathing and nearly unbearable pain. A midwife delivered all of her children at home, but this particular day, she was alone with her one-year-old; the other three children were at school, and her husband, William, was at work. She wondered if she could phone him, but the nearest phone was at a neighbor's house a block away, and anyway, William worked outside the plant welding broken trains—it would take forever to get him to a phone. She continued to watch the clock; she knew the children would soon be home from school.

When the children arrived, they grew disappointed because Margaret, who was usually there to greet them at the door with a hot meal, was lying in bed. They were also all too familiar with the scene; another baby sister or brother would soon make an appearance. Margaret instructed the eldest to go get his grandmother, who lived about a block away. The other children began preparing their meals and caring for the toddler.

William had had a difficult day; regardless of how hard he worked, he could not seem to meet the foreman's expectations. The foreman loomed over him what felt like the entire day. He had the urge to collect and turn in all of his tools and walking out of the plant, but he couldn't just abandon the highest-paying job anywhere in the South. Five dollars was the average weekly salary, yet he made an incredible $37.50. With four children and a fifth one on the way, William couldn't resign, no matter how stressful the job became.

William drove up the narrow, gravel driveway and made his usual right turn in the turnaround. He grabbed his lunchbox and proceeded to enter the house, but before he could open the door, he was greeted by two of the children. In hysterics, they shrieked and pulled him into the bedroom, where he saw Margaret writhing in bed with her mother sitting by her side. He asked how long had she been in pain, but she was in too much distress to answer; instead, her mother explained that she had already labored the entire day but had made no progress. William remembered how difficult the four previous deliveries had been; the last time, he thought he would lose her. William left to get the midwife, who luckily lived only five minutes away. After a brief examination, the midwife recommended the family wait and let Mother Nature take her course; she knew this pregnancy was complicated and far beyond her limited skill.

Shortly after the midwife's departure, Margaret's condition rapidly grew more serious. Her sister's husband, who had come with his wife hoping to meet the new infant, suggested that William should go get his sister, Minnie. A tall, robust woman who had never married, she had assisted many women in delivering their infants; she was not a licensed midwife nor did she have any formal training, but had a natural gift.

By that point, William would have done almost anything to relieve Margaret's agony. He sped off so fast, rocks flew into the air. Minnie lived four miles away, but because there were no paved roads or streetlights, it was a challenge to reach her house. William had to grip the steering wheel tightly to avoid the potholes and to prevent spinning off into a ditch. As he was driving, he worried: what if Minnie were not at home? Perhaps she would be off assisting another family. After all, she was in great demand those days.

Finally, he turned the winding, rocky driveway, and began leaning on his horn as he sped toward the house at the end. Minnie immediately realized someone needed her assistance—after all, this was a frequent occurrence. She snatched her fur coat from the closet, put on a large pair of black boots, and picked up her delivery bag, and before William could even get out of the car, she was hurrying down the front steps. William exclaimed, "Oh, Minnie, come quick! Margaret needs you; she is in so much pain!" They sped back home as quickly as the car would go.

Margaret had moved to the floor by the time they returned; rolling from side to side seemed to ease the pain in her back. Minnie helped her back to bed so she could examine her. She had barely begun to check when she cried, "This baby must be delivered immediately." She ordered Margaret's mother to boil water for her instruments, then gathered towels and placed them at the foot of the bed. Finally, she ordered everyone to leave the room.

One hour later, the loudest cry any of the family had ever heard echoed through the entire house. Everyone rushed into the bedroom, William was in the lead, gasping, "Is it a boy?" Minnie shook her head, smiling. "No, it's a big beautiful, six-pound girl." She handed the proud father his new daughter.

Margaret kept thanking Minnie over and over for saving her life, because she had truly felt as though she were going to die. Minnie just smiled and shook her head as she proceeded to record the date, time of birth, and the sex of the infant in the family's Bible. Suddenly, she turned to Margaret and asked, "What name did you two choose?" Margaret looked perplexed at William, and replied, "We hadn't thought about a name for a girl; we were so sure this baby would be a boy." William thought they should pay homage to Minnie by naming the child after her, but Minnie, refusing to take any such credit, suggested there were other, more suitable names. Margaret suddenly remembered an actress from one of her favorite soap operas, and shyly murmured, "I like the name 'Julie.'" Minnie nodded soberly as she recorded the name. Afterwards, Margaret fell fast asleep.

It was nearly daylight on a blisteringly cold morning, five days before Christmas. William and Margaret would later laugh about receiving an early Christmas present. William was just as exhausted as Margaret; he had been up all night, and now it was time for him to leave for work to prepare for another long, laborious day. Moreover, he would have to go to personnel to report another child as his dependent. He found it somewhat embarrassing, since he had reported a son twelve months earlier, so he decided to wait until the following year to claim another dependent. He asked Minnie to stay with Margaret until he returned from work. Margaret's mother agreed to remain at the house as well, to make the children's breakfast and see them off to school. She had a full-time job and wouldn't be able to come back later that day to help, but before she left, she prepared enough food to last for the entire week. Margaret was resigned to being confined to bed for a week because that was the custom; however, she wished she could just get out of bed to finish baking her traditional pastries. She knew how much William and the children enjoyed her baking, and how much William disliked her mother's cooking—they would often laugh about her mother's poor culinary skills.

The day following the delivery, Margaret finally had the house to herself except for the two youngest children; Minnie had to leave at last, because other families needed her services, and the neighbor (affectionately known as "Prune Face") wouldn't look in on her until later. With no one to chide her, she decided to bake for Christmas after all. While the ten large sweet potatoes were boiling, she began to gather her flour, butter, pecans, sugar, syrup, and other spices. Six hours later, she had baked six sweet potato pies, two pecan pies, one coconut cake, and one chocolate cake. Suddenly, someone knocked on the back door. Margaret knew it had to be Prune Face—*Who else*, she thought, *would stop by at this hour?* She put her robe on over her dress, stacked the used utensils in the sink, and closed the dining room door where the desserts were placed; but, of course, the one thing she could not hide was the aroma of the freshly baked cakes. Prune Face immediately commented on the aroma and asked Margaret if she had been cooking. Margaret could not keep a straight face; she burst out laughing and finally admitted she had completed her Christmas baking. Prune Face was amazed to see the amount of baking she had done, and the old lady shook her head as she cautioned the younger woman to return to bed since her baby was only a day old.

Christmas finally arrived. The children were thrilled with the presents Santa brought them, and Margaret and William looked on and smiled. Julie, only five days old, wanted only one thing—to be nursed every two hours. Margaret went back and forth, meeting the guests instead of remaining confined to bed as was the custom. By and large, Christmas brought great joy to Margaret, William, and their ever-expanding family.

Chapter II

Growing-Up/Pre-School Years

Surrounded by her four older siblings, Julie was forced to grow up rather quickly. She began walking at nine months old. Her brother, almost exactly one year older, felt compelled to protect his little sister. In fact, he stayed by her side constantly. One day while Margaret was preparing dinner, Julie began to cry. Margaret decided to finish one more entrée for the evening meal before returning to the other room to tend to the baby. All of a sudden, there was complete silence. Dismayed and concerned, Margaret rushed to the bedroom, where she was greeted by the toddler. He happily explained he had given the baby something to eat. Margaret rushed to the baby, and realized that the boy had managed to grab some peanuts from a tray in the living room and packed the infant's mouth full of them! Luckily, Margaret managed to remove the peanuts without incident.

A typical day for Julie involved playing from sun up to sun down. She loved to run after the older children, but her favorite activity was pedaling back and forth on her tiny blue tricycle. She was confined to the back yard because the front yard was in close proximity to the main road, where motorists would speed by on a detour from the main highway. One day, Julie decided to shake up her usual routine. She rode her tricycle through the front yard and down the long, narrow driveway. From there, she crept out onto the main road! Just then, a speeding car crested the hill, and as it barreled towards her, she began to pedal as fast as her little feet could go. She flew straight across the road where she landed in a drainage ditch just as the car whizzed by behind her. That event frightened her so badly that she never played in the front yard again.

Most children in the nearby city attended kindergarten, but William and Margaret believed there was no value in sending children to pre-school. Margaret wanted to work, both to maintain her independence and to help earn money for extra amenities for the household. However, William disapproved of her working; he believed a woman's place was in the home, particularly with six children to raise. Margaret couldn't stand just staying home all day, so without William knowing, she worked just a few hours a day for a family who needed someone part-time to do light housekeeping and to serve as a nanny. She would return home just in time to prepare a hot meal for the family. Julie and her younger brother would go to Margaret's sister house while their mother was out at work. Their aunt had once travelled all over the country singing. She was five feet ten inches tall with a very fair complexion, and she thought children with dark complexions were ugly. Julie and her brother had medium- to dark-brown skin, so this aunt thought of them as servants. They were forbidden from being inside unless there was inclement weather; they played outside the entire time.

Once Margaret left and was out of sight, the aunt demanded that Julie empty the disposable bathroom that had sat overnight in the backyard. She would cry each morning as she walked to the end of the yard, knowing that when she opened the lid, she would have to endure the most awful smell of human waste that she could imagine. She would stand there for several minutes, gazing at a distant oak tree from which she took solace from simply gazing at that oak tree because the tree was located at the end of her backyard that brought her comfort. Also she knew it wouldn't be too long before Margaret would return.

Margaret worked only four hours initially so the time appeared to go by rather quickly. After a few months, however, her employer decided to demand that she work a full day. This time, she had no choice but to discuss with William her desire to work. At first he was reluctant, but eventually agreed, provided she would work for only three months. This meant that Julie and her little brother would have to remain an entire day with their aunt. Sometimes William would come home for lunch to check on them. He would bring them a bag of baked peanuts and assure them they would be all right until Margaret returned. It was heartbreaking for Julie to see her father in the middle of the day and then have to watch him go.

Chapter III

First Grade/Cry-Baby

Finally, Julie was old enough to attend first grade. Children in her community and in the surrounding communities rode the bus to school. The bus was so crowded that there were not enough seats for all of the students; some students stood the entire time. This was incredibly dangerous, especially when the bus would stop abruptly. Children would fall on top of each other, or get tossed to the front of the bus. If the children were lucky enough to arrive at school in one piece (which, of course, they did more often than not), they went to attend class in a wooden army barrack. The schoolhouse had old wooden floors, and a large wood-burning stove that sat in the center of the room. There were no bathrooms; when students asked to be excused, the teacher would line them up and lead them to the bathrooms inside the high school across the schoolyard. One day, Julie had to go rather urgently. The day was very rainy and cold, so for once, the teacher allowed her to go alone. As she attempted to navigate a wooden plank crossing a big puddle, she fell and scraped her leg so severely that blood began to ooze from the wound. She began to sob, lying in the puddle, covered in mud and her own blood. Suddenly her cousin, who was in high school, walked by;

she saw Julie crying and ran to her. She assisted her to her feet, then took her inside the school to get first aid, murmuring, "You poor little thing! Now you know why first graders don't go to the bathroom alone!"

First grade was quite an adjustment for Julie; having never attended pre-school, she lacked interpersonal skills. She had a difficult time making friends, and grew sad as her classmates played together without inviting her to join. Her grades reflected this challenge: she made mostly Cs and Ds because she cried almost the entire year.

Chapter IV

Second Grade/The Relocation

The following year, Julie attended second grade in the brand-new elementary school. It had taken years for construction to be completed; several of her older siblings were jealous that they had never had the chance to attend class in the clean and bright new school. By this time, Julie had become adjusted to socializing with other children, riding the school bus, and learning different subjects. Unbeknownst to her, however, she was about to face another setback.

In November, William, along with his co-workers, attended a special call meeting. The supervisor, accompanied by top executives, explained how the company was not as profitable as other plants throughout the country, and so would be closing within ninety days. The employees were given two choices: relocate to St. Louis, Missouri, or to accept a cash payout based on the number years of service. They were given a week to decide. William returned home that same evening, and asked the entire family to join him to discuss what had transpired at work. He and Margaret realized that a payout would not last long as support for their big family, so they had to decide whether the entire family should move, or if he should go alone, leaving the family behind. The family talked for hours, but the children had to go to bed before the decision was made.

The following morning, when the children got up to get ready for school, Margaret and William broke the news: William would relocate alone. He would return home for a visit each month, and during annual inventory. Julie was simply crushed. She began to cry profusely, still crying as Margaret got her dressed before the bus arrived. The bus driver would not wait once the door was closed, even if he saw students running to get on board. Julie couldn't concentrate all day in class as she thought about her father moving away, all alone. Her grades began to decline because she was no longer interested in learning. There were no counselors those days; the teacher simply indicated on her quarterly report card that she needed to improve. Julie, however, barely passed the second grade.

Chapter V

Third Grade/The Reader

Julie finally grew accustomed to William living far away in St. Louis. He came home monthly; sometimes, during a large-scale strike, he would come home for weeks until the strike was over. However, each time he left, Julie would break down and cry. But her grieving was not as prolonged as it had been at first—she would cry for maybe a day or two instead of weeks. Her enthusiasm for learning resumed. She began to read; in fact, she loved to read any book that became available. One day the teacher asked her to stand up and read before the class. She did so, turning page after page; after several minutes, she looked up, seeking the teacher's approval. To her surprise, the teacher was no longer sitting at her desk, but standing in the doorway with another teacher whom she had summoned to witness Julie's exceptional reading skills.

Julie did not realize how her body was changing. She could not understand why it was no longer a good idea for her to run and play without a blouse on during the summer months. One day Margaret asked her to come inside. Once she was inside, Margaret sat her down and instructed her to never play again without a blouse or sweater. Julie was perplexed because her brothers were shirtless. Margaret explained they were boys and she was a little girl, and "girls don't play without wearing a blouse."

She struggled with both math and science because they didn't make sense to her. It didn't help that the classroom was overcrowded: approximately forty students to one teacher, with no time for individual counseling. Her older siblings were busy dating, so they didn't have time to assist her with her homework, and Margaret was no help because she had never completed grammar school. Julie did have a friend who loved math and would try to explain how to solve the math problems. The help didn't seem to matter; Julie found the work much too complex. Eventually, her friend just offered to complete her math assignments. This arrangement would go on throughout grammar school. Luckily, Julie didn't struggle in all her subjects. Although math was challenging for her, she excelled in other subjects such as geography and English, and made it through the grade with good marks.

Chapter VI

Fourth Grade/The Joker

Julie's classmates were much taller and larger than she. Some had been held back as much as two years, while others were just physically mature. Among her classmates was one of her cousins, who often joked around and made her laugh. Unfortunately, this cousin skipped school almost every day. The school was surrounded by dense woodlands, and once recess was over, the cousin and another classmate would hide out in the woods until school was over. The following day, the cousin would return to class, and inform Julie what a great time she had had the previous day. It seemed she really wanted Julie to be a truant as well, but Julie was much too serious about learning; moreover, her upbringing made it almost impossible for her to disobey rules or disrespect those in authority. In the end, Julie stayed in school, while her cousin eventually dropped out. In fourth grade it didn't seem like much, but the tenacity Julie showed for her education would serve her well in life.

Chapter VII

Fifth Grade/Retaliation

Fifth grade was a period of transition for Julie; no longer a child, she entered puberty. She still lagged behind many classmates who had been forced to repeat a year or two; in fact, some of them were taller and larger than the teacher. They were mischievous, uninterested in learning, and attempted on every account to prevent others from learning. The classroom was filled to capacity; as a result, the teacher's role was reversed. Instead of serving as an educator, he policed the classroom in a vain attempt to avoid the almost daily altercations. Most of Julie's classmates traveled to the school from nearby towns. Each group thought its own community was superior to the others, and this led to constant fights and bullying.

Julie was always singled out by the older classmates because she seemed so timid and reserved. One particular day, though, when one of her classmates took her notebook and refused to return it, she had had enough. She jumped up in front of the classroom while the teacher was teaching and screamed as loud as she could, "Give me back my notebook, or I will knock the fire out of you!" From that day forward, she was never victimized again. The teacher never forgot the incident because he commented on her report card that she was pugnacious and had to be forced to do her work. Yet, this was unfounded; she loved to do all her assignments. Perhaps the teacher had gotten her confused with another classmate, but sadly, his comment would remain on her record.

Chapter VIII

Sixth Grade/ The Singer

Julie entered sixth grade with immense enthusiasm, anticipating that she would learn different and exciting subjects. The courses were quite advanced because they were essential to prepare her for high school. Back then, there were no middle schools.

Music was taught in the afternoon. The class was known as the Glee Club, and the music instructor was a perfectionist; she demanded every song was song until there were no flaws, even if it meant staying over after the bell sounded to return to homeroom. She assessed each student's voice. When it was Julie's turn to sing, the instructor determined she sang alto. Julie listened to her sister sing the soprano line, which she loved. So once her group was asked to sing; she shifted from alto to soprano. This would infuriate the teacher. She knew from that time on that singing was not her cup of tea.

The end of the school year came quickly. It was time for the annual Spring Prom. Most of her classmates had friends so they had escorts, but she did not have boyfriends whom she could ask. However, there was one boy who lived in her neighborhood who escorted girls in the community during special events, so she asked him to escort her to the prom. He gladly accepted her invitation. There was only one problem. After the prom was over, this boy demanded a kiss—not to mention how his hands would suddenly become uncontrollable. But she had no one else to ask.

Chapter IX

Seventh Grade/The Haves and the Have-Nots

Seventh grade was pretty exciting. Julie realized the following year she would be entering high school. The courses taught were advanced Algebra, Geography, and science. This was certainly the era to prepare her and her classmates for high school. But there were so many students in the classroom that it was difficult for the teacher to assist a student who may have had difficulty grasping the concept. Moreover, the same teacher taught every course. So if the teacher were not as proficient in one subject area as in another, the students would suffer—especially when the time came to take national college exams. Most of the teachers had graduated from predominantly black colleges nearby, and they would frequently say to students, "I got my education and you have to get yours." Unfortunately, that attitude did not bring success. Instead, some of the teachers stereotyped the students as "unmotivated," " lazy," "an academic failure," and "will never amount to anything in life." Such stereotyping crippled students, especially those who wanted to learn much more than the teacher was capable of teaching.

Julie's experience in the seventh grade could be summarized as an era of recapturing every subject taught from the earlier years. The students could be categorized as "the haves" and "the have-nots." Those who had a solid foundation of the basic fundamentals and an overall understanding of all of the subjects would excel as they entered high school, but students who lacked those basic skills would be ill-prepared for secondary education. As a result, a large majority dropped out of school and never returned.

Chapter X

High School/The Decision

Julie's first year of high school was horrifying because of the number of children enrolled. During recess, the hallway was literally packed. She felt so lost, but once she registered and was assigned to a homeroom class, she recognized some of her elementary school classmates and felt more secure. As the teacher called roll, she realized Julie's older sister was enrolled at the same high school; they looked so much alike, as well as shared their last name. Her sister was quite popular, and the teacher acknowledging the older sister made Julie feel proud. When it came time to leave homeroom to attend the assigned classes, though, Julie once again had to adjust having to meet new classmates. She might have been more cheerful if she had known that she would soon run into her lifelong friend who lived practically next door to the school. They often slept over at the other's house. When Julie saw her, she knew she could relax and enjoy school.

The high school was located in a city known for violence, which often occurred after a Friday night football game. The bullies were usually students who had dropped out of school. Students who were relatively timid or who appeared frightened were easy preys. The bullies would frequently walk up to them and strike them in the face for no reason. During recess, the hallway was so crowded that even students who were enrolled would sometimes get into fights.

Two bells would ring to alert the students that recess was nearly ending: one to warn the students that five minutes remained before class began, and the second to remind them that no one should be left in the halls. But because of the overcrowding, it was impossible for the halls to be vacant even by the time the second bell rang. The school should have been cited due to the number of students that far exceeded the occupancy code. It was by the sheer luck of the draw that there were no major disasters, such as a fire or earthquake. The principal, however, did not take the number of students into consideration when he stood in the middle of the hallway with his belt removed from his pants. If he caught any student in the halls after the second bell sounded, he would lash out at the students as they passed by. He was a very short, skinny man who appeared to be much older than his years. The majority of the students were much larger and taller than he, but they wouldn't dream of retaliating because he frightened the wits out of them.

Julie continued to have difficulties adjusting to high school. The school seemed more like a prison; the children were out of control, deviant, and quite rowdy even during class. She turned all her emotions inward. She never volunteered to speak up in class, even when she knew the answers. As a result, the teacher perceived her as a slow learner, although this was far from the truth. One day her eldest brother, who had graduated some three years earlier, allowed her to wear his class ring around her neck after he had taken the ring back from a former girlfriend. She wore the ring to class, and when the teacher asked for volunteers to read the poem "Whose Woods These Are" by Robert Frost, she volunteered to stand in front of the class to read the poem. The teacher was so surprised; he was almost knocked off his feet. He responded, "Julie volunteered?" He and the entire class were even more impressed when she read the poem with grace and eloquence, meaning and compassion. Complete silence blanketed the entire classroom— most unusual for a room almost always a bedlam.

The end of her second year in high school was drawing near and there were decisions to be made. Her older sister was graduating that year, so Julie could no longer rely on her sister's reputation. Moreover, her brother, who was one year older, decided to transfer to a nearby city high school. This meant if she returned to school the following year, she would be alone. Julie pondered the dilemma, and she began to think long-term. She wondered, because of the school's location and its reputation for violence, if she shouldn't find a better school to attend. She was very wise, even at the age of fourteen, to think of her future. So she decided to follow her brother and transfer to the nearby city school. Of course, even deciding to transfer had its challenges, too. Julie and her brother did not live in the city limits, and lawfully they did not qualify to attend; a dear friend of Margaret who lived in the city decided to allow Julie and her brother to reside with her during the term. This frail, elderly woman lived alone and needed someone to assist her and provide companionship, and the children needed a residence within the city limits. It was a win-win situation.

Chapter XI

City High School/Era of Transitioning

Julie was a sophomore at the time she enrolled at the new city school. The school was much smaller than her former high school; it had only two hundred and sixty students, while her previous school had enrolled approximately twelve hundred. Although the student body was much smaller, one thing both schools had in common was the fact the students seemed out of control during lunch and recess. Still, the students at the city school seemed friendlier and more collegial. They also appeared more mature, willingly complying with the school's policies. Julie felt much more comfortable around this new student body.

Of course, the students and their parents took ownership of this small city school, and were curious whenever new pupils enrolled. The community and school were more like one close-knit family; the parents and teachers visited each other socially, and the principal was a friend of many of the families. But what happened when there were outsiders? Understandably, they were curious about Julie and her brother—and vice versa. There were many whispers, especially among the boys, as Julie walked by on the way to class.

Home Economics was her first class. The teacher, Ms. Boxer, was a relatively short, light-skinned woman of medium build who could easily have been mistaken for a Caucasian or Latina. She had a very down-to-earth demeanor, and she seemed to have a very close relationship with the students, more as a mother figure than an educator. The students sat at a very long table that extended almost to the rear wall of the room, surrounded by sewing machines and one large refrigerator. As Ms. Boxer began to outline the course requirements, she suddenly shifted the conversation to sex education. She began to focus on Julie while warning the class to be wary of "these young boys; all they want to do is throw their trash in your bucket." She continued the conversation with her eyes still fixed on Julie. "Some of you girls are nothing but trash; because you let the boys dump their trash." Obviously, she had obtained some information about Julie being from a nearby town known for violence, teenage pregnancies, and even abortions. It seemed this teacher had stereotyped her before she could even prove herself! She felt very uncomfortable because she realized the long road ahead of her would mean having to prove, not only to this teacher but to the entire student body, that she had had a respectful and decent upbringing. But first, she had to win Ms. Boxer over.

Chapter XII

The Dress Making

As the quarter drew to an end, Julie, who knew nothing about sewing, had not completed making her dress. She was truly about to fail Home Economics. Ms. Boxer had once snatched the material from her in front of the entire class when she failed to trace the pattern correctly; Julie was so embarrassed from that incident that she became afraid to ask for help and instead pretended to be busy pinning the pattern over the fabric over and over. Then one day she decided she would go sit beside Ms. Boxer to chat, because she had learned the importance of engaging her elders in polite conversation. After thirty minutes of chatting with Ms. Boxer, she had won the teacher over. She had her laughing when suddenly the laughing ceased and Ms. Boxer said, "You know we don't have time to waste. We'd better complete your dress." She walked to the table where Julie's fabric was neatly folded, unfolded the fabric, and took a pair scissor to cut the dress from the pattern. After approximately fifteen minutes, she completed making the dress! Obviously, Julie's style and grace won Ms. Boxer over.

The homeroom teacher was a very young man, no more than ten years older than the students. He had grown up in the community, then gone on to complete college and return to teach at the same school from which he graduated. He taught chemistry and biology. He was exceptionally bright and most of the students admired him because of his achievements. One of Julie's close friends had a very serious crush on him. She phoned her each day after school and informed Julie how much she liked the teacher, yet Julie brushed the whole thing off and thought the classmate was delusional.

Julie's homeroom class consisted of students who were not considered as bright as the other homeroom class. But by and large, they stood their ground and earned passing grades for each subject. Moreover, they were respectful of society and would later prove to be productive citizens. Julie was well like by most of them, and she grew sad that when summer came, she would have to say goodbye at least until the end of the summer break.

Chapter XIII

Junior Year City School/Realization

Julie returned to school after the long summer break with enthusiasm and a positive outlook towards the future. She had always wanted to be a professional nurse from the time she was four years old, when she would see advertisements on the back of *True Romance* magazines. As a junior, she realized that in order to be accepted to nursing school, she had to finish high school.

She continued to be a positive role model amongst her peers. Perhaps she went a bit overboard, because she never attended any of the football games or pep rallies, even when the school won a local state football championship title. Ms. Boxer's earlier statement about trashy girls made her more determined than ever to prove she was a decent, moral young woman; as a result, she was never seen at any after-school events. She remained mysterious to the students, and to the teachers.

Literature was taught in the afternoon by a distinguished-looking, average-sized woman, Ms. Banks. She had an incredible, large, hooked nose, and bowed legs which may have been the result of bout of rickets during childhood. Some of the classmates would make jokes about her; moreover, there was another literature teacher down the hall who was more popular because she was much younger, and had a large bust line instead of a large nose. Ms. Banks, however, spoke eloquently and her use of proper grammar and syntax was impeccable; she would not allow students to use what is known today as "Ebonics." She would mimic students if they were caught saying, "I'm fenna," instead of, "I am attempting to." Her method of correcting students was non-intimidating; in fact, the students would laugh at themselves when she corrected them.

Whenever Julie entered a classroom, she moved gracefully, carefully coordinating her movements as she walked across the room and took her seat. In the back of her mind, it was a way to model her ladylike and moral upbringing. Ms. Banks watched her, and afterwards, she asked the class, "Did you all see the way Julie walked in here?" She then proceeded to imitate her. The entire class burst out with laughter, but Julie didn't mind. Obviously, she had impressed Ms. Banks.

Chapter XIV

Twelfth Grade/The Race

Twelfth grade was an era of conformity for Julie. She began to socialize more with her classmates by accepting invitations to birthday parties and group outings; she even accepted one young man's request to go steady. He was a very handsome young man, relatively short with thick, black, curly hair, and he wore glasses that made him look distinguished. He was also exceptionally intelligent. Each Sunday evening, he would come visit her. They would sit in the living room listening to music until eleven o'clock; then he had to leave, because that was the curfew Margaret imposed.

During the second quarter, it was time to elect a "Queen" to represent the school, which meant selecting a candidate from each of the two homerooms classes. The candidate must have had a record of respecting her classmates, passing all her classes, and exhibiting good moral character. Julie was elected unanimously to represent her homeroom class. Happily, she accepted the nomination and promised to represent the class with the highest degree of integrity.

Her first thought was that she needed help writing her campaign speech. She could think of only one individual whom she admired and who, she knew, would have the right degree of eloquence: Ms. Banks of course, Ms. Banks was honored to assist. She guided Julie, informing her about the proper etiquette of public speaking. She should begin by acknowledging the principal, the guidance counselor, and the student body. At the close of the speech, Ms. Banks suggested that Julie recite excerpts of the poem entitled "Self" by an unknown author:

I don't want to rise with the setting sun
And hate myself for the things I've done.
I want to walk with my head erect;
I want to gain all men's respect;
But here in the struggle for fame and wealth,
I want to be able to like myself,
Whether chosen queen or whatever may be,
I will have self-respect and be regret-free.

The study body gave her a standing ovation, but when it came time to count the votes for the school queen, Julie's opponent won in a landslide—one hundred eighty votes to the eighty that Julie received. The students who voted for the opponent explained that they felt they did not know Julie, whereas her opponent was a popular and gregarious girl who socialized with both male and female students. Also, the winner had many supporters who campaigned on her behalf, placing flyers and posters throughout the school campus and neighborhood. Julie lacked that type of support, especially since she was unknown and had only attended the school three years. Yet once the winner was announced over the intercom, she could not hold back the tears. One of the teachers witnessed her obvious emotional breakdown. She approached her with a handful of tissues and said, "You may have lost, but you will always be my queen." *What kind remarks*, Julie thought. She felt someone understood her, that she wasn't alone.

Sadly, she would later report this same teacher to the school's principal. The teacher taught shorthand, and Julie mastered both interpretation and dictation. She made Bs on all the quizzes and exams; however, upon receiving her report card, she received Cs for two quarters. She knew it was erroneous, so she decided to go to the principal to talk to him about this teacher's behavior. Initially, she felt reluctant, thinking the principal might not believe her, given her outsider status. However, she knew the grade was in error, and wanted it to be corrected.

Julie walked into the principal's office anteroom where his secretary sat behind a three-foot-tall wooden counter that almost made her invisible. The secretary asked, "May I help you?"

Julie swallowed and replied nervously, "I would like to see the principal, please."

The secretary got up from her desk and walked into the adjoining office. After a brief moment, she returned and motioned for Julie to enter. She walked into the principal's office, unable to stop her hands from shaking. The principal sat behind a dark mahogany desk; the wall behind him was filled with diplomas and certificates commemorating his many achievements. He reminded her of her father; there was a striking physical resemblance.

The principal wore a dark blue suit, white shirt, and as always, adorned by a colorful dark blue bow tie. In a deep voice, he asked, "How may I help you?"

By now Julie was so nervous she could hardly speak. After a few seconds, she finally responded, "Ms. Alvin gave me Cs on my report card, but I always make Bs." At that point, she was unable to fight back the tears that began to flow down her face.

The principal was silent for a second; then he stood up, walked around his desk, and pulled a chair towards him. He placed his foot in the middle of the chair, cleared his throat, and responded, "Julie, one of the things I caution teachers about during faculty meetings is being jealous of students." She was astonished, stricken with disbelief that a principal would respond in that manner. He went on. "Thank you for bringing this to my attention. I will immediately look into this matter."

From that time on, Julie received Bs on her report card. She was saddened, though, that a student would have to resort to having report a teacher to the principal just to ensure the teacher remained fair and honest.

Julie finally adjusted to losing the race for Queen. One encouraging thing was the school's policy that the individual who lost the title crown would automatically hold the title "Miss Twelfth Grade." Moreover, she began to make plans for the upcoming Senior Prom with her new boyfriend.

Spring came quickly; suddenly, the Senior Prom was two weeks away. She was so excited, knowing she had someone to escort her to the prom; however, her excitement was short-lived. She heard a school–wide rumor that her boyfriend planned to take her to a nearby motel immediately after the prom. She was crushed; she thought he knew that she wasn't a promiscuous girl. So she met with him and informed him she would not be attending the prom with him. He was furious. He made her sit down to itemize all of the expenses he had incurred. She felt remorseful, but she could not take a chance that might tarnish her reputation. On the other hand, she wanted so much to attend the prom, especially since Margaret had purchased her a beautiful, pink and white dress. Suddenly she remembered her old standby, the boy in her neighborhood who was almost always ready to escort girls in the community to any social event. So she asked him, and he accepted.

Many members of the community had gathered outside of the school building to cheer couples as they walked into the prom, as though they were movie stars on the red carpet at the Oscars. Much to her surprise, her boyfriend was standing among the crowd. When it was time for her and her escort to promenade by the crowd, she began to feel as though she would faint. The heels she was wearing suddenly felt as though she were walking on aluminum cans, and suddenly her legs began to wobble. Luckily, she and her escort made it inside, and she breathed a sigh of relief. And unlike the seventh-grade boy with wandering hands, her now more mature escort took her home immediately after the dance ended.

The next school day, countless students approached her commenting about the prom, and how they were surprised to see her with an escort other than her boyfriend. She knew sooner or later that she would have to confront her boyfriend, because she recognized he must have been hurt, as well as teased by so many of his friends. Finally they met in the hallway; they extended each other a cordial greeting and proceeded to go their separate ways. Graduation was near, and the senior year book and other mementos were available. She saw her boyfriend in the hallway, and as a means to amend her past behavior, she asked him to autograph her book. He did more than sign; he wrote a complete page that reads as follows:

Dear Sweetheart,

I could never express this feeling I have for you in words. But I can tell you some very wonderful things that might interest you. Julie, just being able to say you are my girl is an honor to me. Knowing that I am the first means even more. I know that we are two different people. Being that I'm the type that likes to go *a lot* and you being the type that finds better things to do around the house. But believe it or not, you're the type of girl that I really need and really should have, so now you should be able to see why I put up with the things you say and do. Julie, *I* know I'm not the best guy in the world, because I know that there are a lot of things you have heard about me that you consider bad. But you know that there's *some good in everybody* and if given a chance they'll try to prove it, And for you darling I'll try anything, so if given a try I might , well I'm positive that I can prove my point.

Don't think I have forgotten to mention that one thing that all teenage girls (and boys as well) like to hear, Julie: I LOVE YOU. Not one, two, three, or four trillion times, but all the time. When you read the statement above you might say those are just lines; well, just wait until you read what's below. Of all the loves that I've had, you can add them, then multiply them, and still none will compare with yours. Even just to think you love me means more than the world to me. Sweetheart, the left chamber of my heart is for the circulation of blood, but the right one is for the circulation of your love, but one can't operate without the other … so let's hurry and put that right one to work.

Forever and always loving you,

Berry

Chapter XV

Graduation/Farewell

June 2, 1966, was graduation day; this would be the last time Julie would see her boyfriend for a couple of years. He received a scholarship to attend college in Washington, DC, and she was hoping to get accepted at a local college. Unfortunately, prior to the start of the term, she received notice she would have to wait until the second quarter to enroll. She was quite disappointed because most of her classmates had received acceptance letters to attend various universities, yet she was determined to seek other local schools.

Chapter XVI

First Flight/Train Ride

Two weeks after graduating from high school, Julie had another setback. Margaret received a long distance phone call informing her William had taken quite ill, and she needed to come to Chicago right away. (the company closed in St. Louis in the sixties, and William was transferred to Chicago). Margaret was frantic because there was hardly enough money to make ends, meet much less to fly so far; plus, she would have to decide which one of the children should go with her. After all, there were things to consider, such as assisting William physically and attending to a ton of paperwork. After the family congregated, Julie insisted she should be the one to accompany Margaret because the other siblings had jobs and family obligations. Although she tried to protest, Margaret realized it was the most logical option. And so it was decided.

But how would Margaret get the funds to travel? William's brother was one of the richest men in the county; he acquired his wealth by installing septic tanks in countless homes statewide. Margaret phoned him and informed him of William's sudden illness, hoping she could obtain a loan for airfare. He went immediately to the bank, and the following day drove them to the airport.

Neither Julie nor Margaret had ever flown before. The airplane seemed enormous, with at least two hundred passengers on board. Julie had a window seat on the plane. As the airplane ascended, the morning sun was so bright that it nearly blinded her. Once the plane had fully ascended, she began to notice more individuals walking back and forth; some passengers stood in the aisles talking casually, while others were smoking and laughing. She was quite amazed at the calmness and leisurely attitude these passengers had, while she and Margaret were nearly suffered panic attacks.

After only one hour and forty minutes, the plane landed at Chicago O'Hare International Airport. The airport seemed packed with travelers, both domestic and international, but Julie took charge and found a nearby service desk, where the clerk explained how to retrieve their luggage. Afterwards, she flagged down a taxi to take them to the flat that William had rented for nearly thirteen years. The driver was a relatively short, dark African-American man who quickly jumped out of the taxi, opened the door, and motioned as if he were in a hurry. As they slipped into the back seat, he placed their luggage in the trunk and then slammed the trunk so forcefully that it jarred both of them as they sat motionless. As he slid into his seat, the taxi driver asked, "Where to?" Julie confidently replied, "4735 South Michigan Avenue." The driver sped off so fast that Julie and Margaret toppled into each other. They held on tightly as the driver reached a speed of ninety miles per hour, darting in and out of traffic on a busy freeway. Julie had never been in a large city where there were so many speeding drivers who seemed to disrespect each other. Thirteen minutes later, they arrived at the apartment building.

The apartment was in a very old six-story building located on a fairly quiet, tree-lined street. The main outer door was gated like a prison. Next to the door was an intercom system. Once William's landlord confirmed Margaret's identity, a remote system unlocked a second door that let them into the main lobby, where they took elevator to the third floor. There were two large doors that led to the apartments, so they knocked. The landlord opened the door and asked them to enter. The main entrance was a reception area with a large beige sofa and an oversized dark brown coffee table surrounded by an orange Oriental rug that covered the entire room. The odor of the room suggested the carpet had not been cleaned for years.

The landlord's wife led them down a very dark and narrow hallway and to the left. She pointed them to William's room, then returned to the reception area. The room was, sadly, barely more than a closet with a small cart for a bed and a tiny table for William's radio. There was a window; however, the only view was a dirty brick chimney continually belching soot. Julie began to cry for all those years she asked for new shoes and dresses, and the sacrifices he had made to support his family. He selected to live in that small closet in order to save more money to send home to the family.

The day after arriving in Chicago, Julie and Margaret began to make preparations to return home with William. They had flown on a one-way airfare to Chicago, knowing they would return via rail. There was no fee for the train, since William was a railroad employee. It was time to pack all of his belongings, ensuring nothing was left behind; unlike years earlier, when he suffered a stroke and later returned, William would come home for good this time.

The third day, William said his goodbye to the landlord and all of the residents in the apartment building. A taxi drove them to the train station on a very hot day in July. The line to board the train was very long and there was an hour wait before passengers could board. Margaret held on to the carry-on bags, while Julie supported William. Julie realized her father could not stand in line for a long period of time, so she asked Margaret to support him while she ran to the front of the line and demanded assistance from an official. She explained that her father was not only ill, but was also a railroad employee. The head porter followed her to the end of the line where William and Margaret were standing, and instructed the crowd to clear the way to allow them to be the first to board.

The train appeared slow compared to the airplane; it stopped in what seemed like every small town, not to mention the thirty minutes to an hour layover. Moreover, it was very cold inside the train; the air conditioner seemed to be on full blast. Julie asked for extra blankets for William, but he kept removing them.

Julie met a friend on the train in whom she confided her whole life story, especially how she and her mother had come to Chicago to return home with her sick father. The woman seemed attentive, but would frequently leave her seat and would be absent for hours. Julie was perplexed, so one evening when the woman returned asked her, "Where do you go for so long?" The woman just smiled and refused to answer.

Finally, after two days of riding the train, Julie William, and Margaret returned home. Julie arranged beforehand with the porter to authorize William priority in exiting the train. Her eldest brother was at the train station to greet them, and he immediately took charge of pushing William's wheelchair. Shortly after they were settled at home, Margaret managed to get William an appointment to see a neurologist. Upon examining him, the neurologist explained he doubted he would live out the night. Obviously, William had had a cerebral accident (stroke) that resulted in him having weakness on his left side and impaired speech. The doctor prescribed medication and asked that

William have complete bed rest. The news was heartbreaking for Julie and the entire family.

As all of this transpired, Julie was at a crossroad trying to decide whether she should go to nursing school or remain home to take care of William. She agonized about what to do. Amazingly, and in spite of the dire prognosis, William seemed to get stronger every day. Weeks later, Julie received an acceptance to a one-year nursing school. William and Margaret encouraged her to attend.

Chapter XVII

Nursing School/Early Arrival

The family had no money for a four-year nursing program, especially since William was disabled. In fact, there was hardly enough money to pay for medical expenses and to maintain operation of the household. So Julie decided to enroll in a one-year practical nursing program. This would enable her to save sufficiently and later enroll in a professional nursing school.

In the fall of 1966 she began the program. The school could easily been mistaken for a cathedral. The building was made up of dark red bricks with white marble skillfully crafted along the side, and a large clock embedded in the facade that overlooked the main interstate. Students who depended on public transportation had to walk approximately one mile on a winding, wooded, narrow path before they could gain access to the school campus. This was very dangerous during early fall for nursing students, because most of the classes began at 7:00 a.m. Julie and her classmates met each morning to walk together, but if she overslept, she would have to take a later bus, and would have to walk the trail alone. She realized the danger of walking alone because it was reported one woman was raped in the same vicinity. She had to be dressed to leave at five in the morning in order to ride the 5:15 bus. The bus would take her downtown, where she would transfer to a second bus that went all around the city and finally to the outskirts where the nursing school was located. The entire community was asleep when she left to attend school, except for one neighbor who would be up watering his lawn in the glow of the flood lights. It was comforting to her to know someone else was starting his day as early as she.

The nursing instructor was a short, plump young woman with a noticeable gap in between her teeth. She had one daughter of whom she spoke often during her lectures. Obviously, this daughter was the most precious individual in this teacher's life. Julie noticed that the instructor never mentioned having a husband, she never wore a wedding ring, and she never talked about being married. She was quite stern and focused, and felt strongly that she needed to ensure each student received adequate lesson materials in preparation for the four quarterly National League of Nursing Examinations and the State Board of Nursing Examinations for licensure. It was most important to her, and she took it personally that a neighboring school had a higher success rate of students passing the national exams and state boards.

The first quarter included basic anatomy and physiology; Julie found two hundred six bones and five hundred muscles in the human body most intriguing. She returned home each evening to share with Margaret and William what she learned that day. She saw how proud both were of her having decided to attend nursing school. She prayed constantly that William would live to see her graduate and to become a nurse.

Theory taught in the classroom was one thing, but theory in application was another. Two days a week, she and her classmates were assigned patients at the hospital—no more than two, but two who required a lot of nursing care. The hospital was the largest public hospital in the city, where the sickest patients were admitted. The majority of them were uninsured and fell far below the poverty line; therefore, they could not afford annual physical examinations or any other disease prevention measures. The patient assessment began at 7:00 a.m. and the students' assignments were to be completed by 11:30 a.m. That meant bathing the patients, changing the beds, performing and documenting all treatments, and reporting on the patient's condition to the staff nurse all had to happen before the one-hour lunch began . After lunch, the students would attend a four- hour lecture in a classroom at the hospital. One day Julie was assigned to an elderly patient who had sustained third-degree facial burns after a chemical she was using to clean a gas oven ignited. The complete right side of her face was blown off, exposing the uvula, muscles, tendons, and tongue. A sterile gauze patch was the only thing covering the hole. Julie had to irrigate the hollow area every two hours without allowing the irrigation apparatus to touch any of the exposed parts. The staff nurse removed the patch to demonstrate the technique further, and noticed that unlike so many other nursing students, Julie looked on without any reaction. She knew that, as a professional, she must be strong and empathetic regardless of any condition she encountered. But this poor woman was a horrible sight to look at, and it was terrifying having to see half of her face missing. She irrigated the wound just as instructed, gave her report to the staff nurse at the end of the practicum, and left to attend class. Suddenly, in the middle of the class, the hospital administrator interrupted the instructor. She apologized for the disruption but explained that the patient was refusing to allow anyone other than Julie irrigate her facial wound; happily surprised, the instructor dismissed Julie to attend to her patient. It was one of the first of many examples of her professionalism and loyalty to the nursing profession.

Just before she turned eighteen, Julie graduated from the program —four months too young, in fact, to take the State Board of Nursing for Licensed Practical Nurses exam. As soon as she turned eighteen, she took the state examination and passed with a very high score. Remarkably, William lived to see his youngest daughter's dream come to fruition.

Chapter XVIII

The Work Force

Julie accepted a full time position as a Licensed Practical Nurse at the hospital where she had trained. Most of her classmates worked the night shift, so on the day shift she met many new people. She vowed she would never work the night shift on a full-time basis because she believed in order to be an effective nurse, she had to have eight hours of night sleep.

Her first assignment was an eight-bed medical intensive care unit. The head nurse was a very young nurse who apparently went to nursing school simply to meet and marry a doctor. This was a teaching hospital with many interns, residents, and attending physicians. Each month a different team of interns and residents were assigned to the intensive care unit, and the young head nurse flirted with many physicians. Sometimes she would go have coffee with them, leaving the heavy task of the overall patient care to Julie and a staff nurse. Both of them worked so hard that at the end of the day they could hardly walk to their cars to drive home. Julie quickly learned the intensive care unit routine; although, as a Licensed Practical Nurse, there were restrictions on procedures she was allowed to perform, there was still much that she could do. For instance, she could administer oral medications, record intravenous fluid levels, to the patients. However, there were many occasions when the staff nurse was ill or recruited to work in another area of the hospital, and she was left with only the head nurse to help care for eight critically-ill patients. During those times, Julie would often perform restricted tasks because the head nurse was ill-prepared to do so. For example, she assisted when there were cardiac arrests; in fact, newly-assigned registered nurses depended on her to train them during emergencies.

At the end of one long day, she was heading out when, to her surprise, she saw her former high school boyfriend. He had been visiting a family member. They both smiled and embraced each other. He was equally surprised to see her working in her career after only two years of graduating from high school; he mentioned that he had dropped out of school for personal reasons. She insisted upon driving him home, and on the way they chatted about old classmates until suddenly the conversation ceased. As they sat in silence, Julie couldn't help but notice how hyperactive he was, to the point of appearing nervous and preoccupied. After twenty minutes, she arrived at his home. He thanked her and said goodbye.

That would be the last time she would see him; he died some thirty-four years later.

Chapter XIX

Return to School/Nursing

Two years after working as a full-time nurse, Julie began to assess her skills and annual salary. She compared her salary to that of a registered nurse, and discovered that salary was twelve thousand dollars more. Given that she did most of the work anyway, she decided to continue her nursing training and become a registered nurse. She continued to save as much money as she could, but her savings were insufficient to attend the college of her choice. So she decided to attend a local two-year community college during the summer of 1970. She knew she needed to concentrate totally on her studies; therefore, she resigned from the hospital when she started school. She was fortunate to have a place to live; by living with her parents, she didn't have to worry about paying monthly rent, and so could leave her job without too much concern.

She started classes at the community college, but quickly became discouraged after talking with many students who explained how difficult it was to get accepted into the actual nursing program. Some had been waiting as long as five years. Julie had no desire to wait seven years before completing nursing school. She began to ask more questions. Who decided who would get accepted into the program, and what were the prerequisites? One student gave her the name of a woman who was in charge of Admissions. At that point, Julie realized she faced two major hurdles: figuring out how she would complete the required academics, and meeting and winning over this woman who held the key to her future.

The following week, she phoned the Admissions Office and asked for an appointment. The secretary gave her a date with three different times and asked which she preferred. Surprised, she quickly selected the time that worked best with her schedule. The secretary cautioned her that numerous students made appointments and failed to keep them; if she failed to keep the appointment, she might never get another one. But Julie wasn't about to give up; she was determined to do whatever it took to get into the nursing program. Besides, she had worked in the industry and knew how important it was to achieve a higher nursing degree.

The day of the appointment, she was quite nervous. Obviously, this woman had interviewed many students; Julie had no idea how she made the decision either to accept them into the program or to keep them on the waiting list until they finally gave up. Julie walked into the office, introduced herself, and informed the secretary she had an appointment. The secretary looked at a calendar to confirm the appointment; then she got up and asked Julie to follow her.

Julie was escorted into a large office painted very light beige, with long floral drapes on the windows. Seated behind a huge mahogany desk was a gray-haired woman who appeared to be in her seventies. She had a stoic, serene look as the secretary introduce Julie to her; in fact, she reminded Julie of her grandmother.

As soon as the secretary left, the woman asked, "So tell me ... why you decided to become a nurse?" Julie explained it had been her dream since the age of four to become a nurse. She shared how she had recently graduated from practical nursing school and had passed the State Board of Nursing Exam for Practical Nursing with high marks.

After thirty minutes, the elder woman explained that there were over five hundred students on the waiting list, and the next nursing class began in two months. She then looked Julie straight in the eyes and asked, "Are you passing your classes?"

Julie had been raised to respect her elders, and she met the woman's gaze as she responded, "Yes ma'am, I am."

The woman continued, "Then I will approve your acceptance into the nursing program." Julie knew this was contingent upon her passing all of her classes for the current quarter, but she was still ecstatic. Additionally, the admissions director authorized a $1,200 stipend to be issued quarterly to assist in the purchase of books. Julie could not hold back her tears as she stood up to thank the admissions director for believing in her.

That evening, Julie told her parents about the older woman who, in her opinion, had made her dream come true. Margaret and William were thrilled to hear she had been accepted into nursing school. Julie did caution them that her acceptance was contingent on her passing her classes that quarter, and that the writing course was a bit difficult; however, William was confident she would pass. Julie was determined to prove him right and make him proud.

Julie studied harder than ever because she knew her lifelong dream was at stake. Unfortunately, she continued to fail her English Composition class. Julie prayed continually, but she was beginning to feel defeated. Recalling how she had developed a rapport with her Home Economics teacher, she thought she would try to develop a relationship with the English Composition instructor. One day after class, she approached the teacher and commended her for her superb teaching technique, and how she made the theory of writing very clear, but admitted that because of her earlier schooling, she was not proficient in her writing skills. The teacher stood motionless, her skin reddening. Julie explained how hard she was trying to be a good writer, and asked if she could practice by doing extra writing assignments; she also confessed her hope that the teacher would assist her in reviewing her writing outside of the regular class assignments. The teacher appeared to be in a state of shock. Finally, she responded, "Yes, I would be more than happy to help you."

Weeks after the conference, Julie noticed a change in her grades. There would be corrections and suggestions on her writing assignments, and her final grades were no longer Ds but Cs. Moreover, she continued to turn in extra writing assignments. When final exam time came, she felt confident she would pass all of her courses, although she was still less confident about English Composition. The exam consisted of three parts: multiple choice, true or false, and a three-paragraph essay on one of three topics. She took her time answering each question, and when it came to the writing portion, she remembered all of the rules of correct punctuation and grammar. After one hour, she turned in her exam paper feeling anxious and overwhelmed, but hopeful.

Two days later, it was time to see the final exams for the ending quarter. The grades were posted outside of the building. The students' social security numbers were recorded to identify each student and the grade was recorded next to the social security number. Julie drove to the college to determine her fate, but she could not find a parking space. She drove around and around the parking lot, growing more and more anxious until she broke out into a cold sweat. When she finally parked, she was tempted to run to the building, but she gathered her composure and began walking calmly, despite her heart pounding.

As she approached the first building where her sociology grade was posted, Julie saw that a large crowd of students had gathered to view their grades. Each student approached the door of the building, viewed his or her grade, and turned to leave—so the line moved relatively quickly. Julie was pleased to find she had earned a B, but knew there were other buildings remaining. She had to keep going before she knew if she had passed all her classes.

The second building was where the political science grades were posted. There were a few students outside, but they were not in line, so Julie was able to go immediately to the glass door to see that her final grade was a B. She should have been pleased, but she still could not celebrate. Her next stop was the science building, where she found a very long line. After twenty minutes, she found she had made a B for anatomy and physiology.

There was nothing else now; she had to head to the final building, the English Department. As she walked, she began to wonder all of her efforts would pay off. *What if she did poorly on the final exam? What if her cumulative score did not average to an overall passing score?* All sorts of things raced around her mind as she walked towards the south college campus. Strangely, there were no crowds standing in front of the English building's door; there was only one student viewing her grade, and she quickly stepped aside to allow Julie access.

Julie grew more nervous as she tried to locate her social security number; the longer she looked, the more her vision blurred. She saw many Fs on the list, which caused her heart to race so much that she felt as though she would faint. Finally, she saw her number and next to it, in big, bold ink, a C. She jumped and let out a shout; she couldn't have been happier if she had received an A. She knew she was officially accepted into the nursing program for the following quarter; once again, her dream and prayers were answered.

She began the nursing program in the fall of 1970. The first quarter was basic nursing, which covered how to take vital signs, proper bed-making technique, and developing individual patient treatment plans. This class was a review for her since she was a licensed Practical Nurse. The class was only four hours long, and afterwards, most students went home to study and to complete their homework assignments; however, Julie remained on campus to attend other classes. Unlike the majority of the other students, who had taken all of the required academic courses, she was taking a full load of twenty hours. But she did well, passing all of her classes during that first quarter with a 3.5 grade point average.

Second quarter was advance nursing and required more clinical work, so the students were assigned to the hospital three days a week. Each was assigned one patient. Julie was far more advanced clinically than her classmates, so the instructor assigned her three patients. She found the second quarter to be easy and enjoyable, especially since they were required to stay only four hours. The hospital was less than a mile from her home, so at the end of the clinical training, she had the opportunity to return home to check on William. Since Margaret was forced to return to work to assist in paying medical bills, William spent the days home alone.

One day as Julie was driving home from the hospital, she noticed a strange, dilapidated truck parked in front of her home. She parked and entered the house, expecting to see William sitting in the recliner as usual. Instead, she found him in the bedroom with all his rare coins spread out, showing his collections to a complete stranger. This stranger stood over him as he was counting and carefully lining up each coin on the bed. The stranger appeared to be in his late seventies; his attire was relatively sloppy and dirty, and from the looks of his old truck full of odds and ends, he was probably a junk man.

As Julie entered the bedroom, both of them jumped at her sudden appearance. She asked William in a hostile tone, "Just what are you doing?"

The stranger obviously felt his presence was not welcome and piped up, "I better be going." He hurried out the door. Julie turned to William and scolded him for having a complete stranger inside their home. She noted the danger involved, especially since he was weak from having a previous stroke, and explained how this man could have assaulted him. "What if he had taken all your coins? No one ever would have known what happened, and we would never have gotten them back!" she cried.

William sat like a little child as she went on and on. When she finally stopped, murmured, "You're right, honey. That man could have hurt me. I won't do it again; you know, whenever someone tells me something for my own good, I listen." The man was never seen again and William never invited anyone else inside the home again.

It was clear that Julie had taken on the role more of a mother figure than as a daughter. Since William's illness, she had become overly protective of him. Each time she saw him working in the yard, cutting the shrubs with manual clippers, she ordered him to sit in the shade while she completed the task; she knew he shouldn't exert himself. One day he commented to her, "You should have been a boy." Julie didn't mind; she would do any masculine task to prevent him from having another stroke. She truly loved him.

Chapter XX

Graduation/Blind Date

Julie satisfied the required coursework and graduated from nursing school in eighteen months, earning the right to sign her name as "Julie, Graduate Nurse." Ironically, graduation was held on the same date she graduated from Practical Nursing School two years earlier, August 22. William and Margaret were so proud of her. William attended the graduation ceremony; he had longed for that day to see her march with over two hundred graduates. Moreover, out of ten African-American students who entered the nursing program with her, she was the only one who graduated in such a timely fashion. Her dream was fulfilled and, more than that, her prayers were answered: again, William lived to see her graduate.

After graduation, she returned to the same public hospital where she had worked previously. Being employed at this particular hospital meant she did not have to repay the federal loans, because the hospital was considered an approved site serving an underprivileged area. Also, this was the hospital that had inspired her wonder as a child. Each time that Margaret drove her and her siblings downtown, she would stop and stare at the nurses dressed in their white uniforms with their navy blue capes draped on their shoulders. Her eyes would illuminate with admiration as she watched.

The next hurdle was passing the National Professional Nursing Standard Board Exam in two months. Each evening after returning home from work, she studied in preparation. William and Margaret felt confident she would do well. She was anxious because the exam would cover all aspects of nursing, and nursing students who had graduated from a four-year college would sit in for the same exam. She began to worry that her school was deficient and had failed to cover most of the material, or that she had forgotten most of the theory and concepts. But she continued to review the study guides and notes each evening.

A week before the examination, she received an official notice of the testing site and instructions, such as what to bring, what was forbidden, and an overview of samples of the examination. The morning of the exam, she was nervous as she entered the building to sign in, looking at the crowd of students; there had to be nearly two hundred of them. Each was directed a designated classroom. The exam started at 8: 00 a.m. for the first portion and concluded at noon. The second half began at 1:00 p.m. Once the day of testing ended, she felt completely drained, and a good night's sleep didn't seem to help. She returned to work the following day, exhausted. She worked in a diabetic crisis unit where patients were admitted whose blood glucose was elevated as high as 1000 milligrams (normal glucose level ranges from 80 to 120 milligrams), There were many admissions that day, as well as transferring patients out to the adjoining ward and quickly preparing to take care of the new admissions. Somehow she made it to the end of the day, despite her fatigue.

Six weeks later, Margaret called Julie at work to tell her she had received a brown envelope from the state. Knowing it was the results, Julie asked Margaret to place the envelope on her bed. She could hardly work that day thinking about the letter and whether or not she passed the examination. The day seemed to drag by because there were very few admissions and hardly enough to do. Finally, her eight-hour tour was over. She left the ward hurriedly, not pausing to chat with the incoming nurses as she usually did. When she got home, she ran into her bedroom and opened the letter. The letter outlined each of the nursing areas, the average score, and the candidate's score. She passed; her license was affixed to the second page. Julie screamed so loudly that it startled her parents, who came running. When she grinned at them and showed them she had passed her exam, they laughed and clapped. Julie was thrilled that she now could sign her name as "Julie, RN."

Most days after she returned home, Julie would sit and chat with William, who was a philosopher in his own right. He would sit and talk for hours with the children in the community, advising them how to live morally and reminding them of the importance of respecting one another. Julie had learned this lesson well. When she was in nursing school, she had tutored an elderly classmate who had difficulty passing one of her classes. The older woman's husband would drive her and would wait in the car while Julie tutored her. William seized the moment to strike up a conversation with this man, who obviously enjoyed engaging in lengthy conversations. Both father and daughter treated the elders of the community with the respect they had earned.

William became concerned about Julie not having a social life. So one day, he began a serious talk with her. He first explained to her how his sister, Minnie, who had delivered her, had never married, and how eventually she developed depressive, antisocial behavior. William encouraged Julie to socialize more with her peers, to start dating—he urged her to live her life. Julie was quite content to work each day and then return home to Margaret and William, but to please her father, she eventually started going to movies with some of the nurses after work, and occasionally the charge nurse would invite her over for dinner.

The family attorney's secretary was very fond of the family, especially William who had to meet with the attorney one day, and Julie and the secretary started a conversation. Julie shared that William wanted her to marry. The secretary perked up at the chance to play matchmaker, talking about a client whom she described as "a handsome young man" who recently divorced. She cautioned Julie that she could not violate client-attorney confidentiality, so she would simply ask the young man if he would be interested in meeting a friend of hers.

Two weeks later, on Monday evening, Julie received a phone call from this young man. They talked until midnight and, eager to meet each other, agreed that he would come to her house the following Sunday. Julie fretted over what to wear, finally choosing casual slacks and a beautiful blue blouse. The young man arrived around eight in the evening. Margaret greeted him and asked that he be seated while she got Julie. As Julie entered, she was pleasantly surprised to see a tall, handsome man in a beautiful tweed suit, and white shirt, and a brown and blue tie. He wore glasses, which made him look more distinguished. The two of them talked and listened to music until nearly eleven o'clock, which was Julie's curfew. He promised to phone her once he arrived home, which he did. They talked well past midnight, despite both of them having to report to work relatively early the following day.

The second time he visited, she decided to dress in a more modern style, so she went to her favorite store, Saks Fifth Avenue, and purchased a short beige skirt, a beautiful brown turtleneck sweater, and dark suede boots. When she walked in the room, his eyes widened and his mouth spread into a glowing smile. He commented on how beautiful she looked, and told her she looked better each time they met. They discussed her desire to marry and to raise a family; however, he vowed he would never remarry after having gone through a long and bitter divorce—he had to pay such a substantial amount of money to hire an attorney that he hardly had sufficient funds to take her out to a movie. The court awarded the house to his ex-wife, forcing him to move into his parents' basement. Julie understood, but thought maybe one day he would change his mind, and she would be the one he would choose to marry.

After a year and a half, she asked William for his opinion of her young man. Oddly, William, who was always watching her and all of her associates, could not give her his take on the young man. Although he spoke to her beau each time he visited, William admitted he hadn't had the opportunity to observe the young man. Julie left the conversation thinking that William's behavior was quite unusual.

Approximately one month after Julie and William conversed about her boyfriend; William took ill and had to be hospitalized. She began to think perhaps he had not taken time to observe her beau carefully because he had not felt well, but didn't want anyone to know the severity of his illness.

Chapter XXI

The Funeral/ The Losses

William underwent major abdominal surgery twice in six months. He was recuperating after the second surgery and was scheduled to be discharged the morning that he died. Julie working when a call came; William had taken a turn for the worst. She hurried to the third floor of the hospital, but as she approached his room, she noticed a yellow tape draped on the door. She removed the tape and entered the room, where she saw him lying in bed as though he was asleep. She began to cry, rubbing his forehead, but he wouldn't wake up. The phone was on the nightstand and the first person she phoned was her boyfriend. She wept as she told him William had died.

That night was a very sad night for Margaret, Julie, and all of Julie's siblings. Surprisingly, Julie's boyfriend came to console her, and to be with the family. She was so grateful he came during a time of need. Many neighbors and distant relatives also came to console the family. However, there was a lot of planning to do, including making the funeral arrangements and gathering all of the legal documents. Julie's boyfriend only stayed a short while, although promised to phone her later that evening.

Margaret tried to be strong during the funeral, and asked Julie and the rest of the siblings to do the same. Julie's boyfriend held up his promise and accompanied her to the funeral. Unbeknownst to her, though, she was about to be confronted with another loss. After the funeral, her boyfriend sat down and talked with her about being strong for Margaret in the days ahead; he went on to tell her that he had recently purchased a home nearby and felt he needed time to be free. He explained he was not accustomed to just sitting with someone on Sunday nights; he was ready to go out and live his life again. Julie was crushed. She felt the whole world had come crashing down on her. She cried profusely the entire night.

Julie returned to work the following week. Work kept her occupied, and by the time she came home in the evenings, she was exhausted. The demands of being a nurse helped her to get through her loss of both William and her boyfriend. Moreover, she had to ensure Margaret was all right as well. She continued to take her work seriously, and was loyal and dedicated as well as committed to upholding the highest standards of the nursing profession.

Chapter XXII

The Doctor/The Admirer

Julie's dedication and hard work paid off, because the director of
one of the outpatient clinics was seeking to hire a registered nurse in
one of the most prestigious clinics in the hospital, the Cardiac Clinic.
This clinic was endorsed by a local radio station; the director of the
clinic would appear monthly as a guest to answer calls from listeners
throughout the state regarding heart disease and prevention. Patients
who had undergone coronary bypass surgeries would attend classes
on proper nutrition and exercise taught by the nurses in this clinic.
There were five nurses assigned to the clinic, and they rotated monthly
among the assignments. One would teach the classes; another would
oversee the clinic to ensure patients were registered; two would assist the
physicians; and another would conduct video training for the patients
as they waited to see the doctor. Julie was incredibly proud to be part of
such a prestigious clinic. Moreover, being employed there proved to be
therapeutic; she soon forgot her break-up thanks to being surrounded
by so many friendly co-workers who would frequently invite her to their
homes for dinner.

When it was Julie's turn to conduct the four-week class in the hospital, she entered a patient's semiprivate room. She noticed the curtains were drawn and realized a physician was examining the patient in the next bed. She introduced herself to the patient in the first bed, and explained she would be his teacher for the next four weeks. She gave him an overview of the class; afterwards, she paused to allow him to ask questions. After she finished and was saying goodbye, a voice suddenly echoed from behind the curtains, "Julie, is that you?" The curtain was pulled back, and there stood a tall, handsome physician who was doing his residency training. Julie stared at him with dismay as he continued, "How have you been?"

She was perplexed because she did not know him, but he obviously knew her. She played along and cordially replied, "I am just fine, thank you, Doctor." She walked out of the room and went about her day, soon forgetting the incident.

The following day, however, she was greeted by the same physician. He asked if he might refer one of his patients. She smiled and thanked him for the referral. She had a full class to teach that day, not to mention having to transport some of the patients who were dependent on wheelchairs back to their rooms. Returning the heavy equipment back to the clinic was quite a chore, but Julie loved every minute of her work. At the end of the day, although she was fatigued, she looked forward returning .

The third day Julie, as usual, began her day by gathering all of the teaching materials. She stopped briefly to chat with the nurses in the clinic. Their chatting was mostly small talk: TV programs, family matters, boyfriends. After her brief chat she headed to the hospital floor, where she realized immediately it was going to be an unusually busy day because of the numerous physicians who had gathered around the desk. Moreover, another group of physicians were making rounds in the middle of the hallway, and there were even more physicians in the doctors' conference room. The congestion would make it nearly impossible for her to obtain the patients' medical records, which were essential for documenting the patients' progress.

First she went to the medical record chart stand to locate the patients' records; however, none of the records she needed were present. She then proceeded to enter the doctors' conference room; there, she found several doctors reviewing charts, while a great number of medical records were left scattered about the table. She became hopeful she would find some of the records she needed and began to sort through the charts on the table. Suddenly, the physician whom she had met earlier grinned and remarked, "Julie, the most beautiful girl in the hospital." She looked up at him and smiled, but merely continued to look for records so she could get on with her day.

She finally found some of the charts she needed and turned to leave the room. The young physician ran after her and gave her another referral to see one of his patients; it turned out to be the same one he had given her before. She brushed it off, thinking perhaps he had forgotten; it was easy for doctors to lose track of some of their referrals, and she knew the resident was quite busy.

Julie later returned to the clinic and found everyone had left for the day except for the clerk. It had been an exceptionally long and hectic day, starting with the search for the charts and then having to teach a class of more than ten patients. She was waving goodbye to the clerk when he looked up and said, "Oh, don't leave yet, Julie; you have a phone call."

That's odd, she thought, since she informed Margaret she would be home later than usual. She began to think maybe something had happened to her mother, so she quickly turned around and answered one of the main phones in the clinic.

At first there was silence, but then a voice said, "Julie, this is Dr. Clark. Will you go out with me tonight?"

On the other end of the phone, Julie smiled. Without hesitation, she replied, "Yes." He asked for her address, but instead, she suggested they both meet at a nearby plaza that was a halfway point for both of them. "I'll see you there, Dr. Clark," she finished, and hung up the phone.

Julie could hardly believe she had consented to going out with this physician whom she barely knew. *Why am I doing this?* She asked herself. Of course, she knew it was about time to break the routine and stop reminiscing about her former boyfriend. But now she had to rush home shower, change clothes, style her hair, ensure Margaret had dinner, and drive to the plaza within two hours.

At home, she discovered Margaret had cooked, but she explained she was going to skip their usual sit-down dinner because she was going out with a friend. Margaret was pleased that she was finally going out on a date. She had watched her daughter over a period of months as she grieved over both William's death and the break-up with her boyfriend. Julie rolled her hair, took a shower, and after going back and forth managed to select slacks and a short-sleeve blouse with a matching vest. She arrived on time and expected to see him standing in front of the plaza, but she did not see him. Moreover, she didn't know what type of car he owned, and he did not know the type or model car she drove. She decided to park her car and stand in front of the plaza to give him an opportunity to recognize her, but after five minutes of pacing back and forth with her shoulder bag dangling off her shoulder, she decided to go inside. The waiting area overlooked the parking lot, which gave her a direct view of motorists entering and exiting. After fifteen minutes past the hour, she decided to phone the hospital to page him; of course, the operator explained he failed to respond the overhead page and had undoubtedly left for the day. She went back to the front of the plaza, and less than a minute after returning saw a shiny red convertible sport car driving far beyond the speed limit. She looked and it was Dr. Clark at the wheel, smiling and waving for her to join him.

As she got inside the car, he began to apologize for being late and went on to explain how a patient's condition had worsened. He asked if she would mind if he went to home to check his mail before they started out for dinner. She smiled, and responded, "Of course not." He headed down a quiet street surrounded by condominiums and apartment buildings where mostly single professionals resided. He then made a right turn into his apartment complex, which was very upscale. He drove slowly, pointing out a tennis court, a large swimming pool, and clubhouse. Finally, he parked and, leaving keys in the ignition, he darted out and ran down some stairs to an area that contained each tenant's secured mailboxes. Julie watched from the car as he perused each correspondence carefully, as if he was expecting something very important. Then he opened his apartment door, tossed the mail inside, and returned to the car. He asked what type food she preferred. Julie wasn't a big eater so she replied, "A salad would be lovely."

He replied, "I know just the place."

They drove to the next small town, to a steak and seafood restaurant. The restaurant was considerably crowded despite the fact it was a weeknight. Once they were seated, the waiter gave them a menu and asked if they wanted to order a drink. Dr. Clark ordered a beer for himself and wine for Julie. They talked about a lot of different things while they ate. She explained about the breakup between her and her boyfriend, and the death of her father one year earlier. He sat and listened intently; his eyes never wavered to look at anyone but her. It was as if no one else existed. She admitted to him that she did not remember him as he rotated in the hospital. He explained that, as an intern a year earlier, he watched her take care of his patients and wanted to ask her out, but was too afraid to ask.

When it was her turn to ask questions, she learned he had a younger sister and an older brother. Later she attempted to guess his hometown, but was unsuccessful. She learned he grew up in Seattle, Washington. He thought it was extremely important for her to refer to him by his first name, Jeremy, but while they were in the hospital setting, she could refer to him as Dr. Clark. She asked if there was a special someone in his life. He confessed there was a young lady in his hometown who had been his childhood sweetheart, and she was waiting for him to marry her. Then he suddenly changed the subject.

They ate steak, baked potato, and salad, then went to the adjoining room to hear a live band. The music was a mix of country, pop, jazz, and western. Everyone seemed to be enjoying themselves. Julie didn't much care for the music, but after having a second glass of wine, she found it tolerable. She and Jeremy laughed and held hands as if they had known each other all of their lives. But it was late in the evening, approaching 11: 00 p.m. on a weeknight, and both had to be at work early the following day, so they called it a night. On the way back, she joked and teased him, while ruffling his hair as he drove. She joked about the relatively obese nurses in the hospital having a crush on him. They laughed all the way back to the plaza, where her car was the only car left. He was surprised to see the shiny blue Corvette; William had given her the down payment as a gift for graduating from nursing school. He commented how the car was much too big for such a little girl like her. Still smiling, they bid each other good night.

Driving home, Julie thought how much fun she had had, and realized how much she missed going out. She feared she couldn't get serious about Jeremy because he was already promised to marry his hometown sweetheart, though, she vowed never to go out with him again. Yet on the other hand, she couldn't dismiss the fact he made her feel special in a way no one else ever had.

Margaret was still up waiting for her. She wanted to know if her daughter had had a nice time, and she had many questions regarding this young doctor's upbringing. Julie was too tired to engage in a lengthy conversation, but promised to fill her mother in on all of the details the following day.

It seemed as though she had just gotten into bed when she was awakened by the alarm clock. She dragged herself out of bed slowly, but finally made it to the bathroom to take a hot shower. Before heading out the door, leaving, she went into Margaret's bedroom to say goodbye. Margaret had had a very late night too, waiting up for Julie, usually she would be up talking to her as she prepared to go to work, but today she had slept in. They promised to chat that evening.

Julie arrived to work on time and, as usual, she stopped to chat briefly with the other nurses. One of them asked her about her evening, and she smiled, saying only, "Oh, I had fun; I went out with a friend for dinner." No one asked whether the friend was female or male and she was not going to say one way or another. She waved her goodbyes and proceeded to the patient area of the hospital.

Julie hoped she wouldn't run into Jeremy that day, because she was slightly embarrassed for laughing and acting completely out of character the night before. She decided to go to a different floor first; hopefully, by the time she made it to his floor, he would have conducted rounds and left to go to the outpatient clinic. It was mid morning before she made it to his floor; confident he must have left, she picked up referrals and began to walk with the patients to the classroom. Suddenly, a voice from behind said, "Good morning, Ms. Julie." She looked around ... and there was Jeremy. She smiled and replied, "Good morning." She didn't stop to talk, though, and moved on with the patients to the classroom.

Afterwards, she was paged by one of the nurses in the clinic to assist due to the number of unscheduled patients. She hurried over, and found that there were so many patients waiting outside the clinic that they were leaning against the wall. She quickly put her teaching materials away so she could assist the patients. There was much to do: placing them in the exam rooms, assisting the physicians during physical examinations, administering medications, and drawing blood. But at the end of the day, every patient had been seen. Relieved, Julie was ready to head home, when she heard that one of the nurses had taken ill and would not be allowed to return to work until the following week. That meant the inpatient teaching for that week was canceled, and she would remain in the clinic. She couldn't decide if she was pleased or disappointed that she would have little chance to see Jeremy.

He, however, was obviously hoping to see her. When she didn't appear on his floor, he paged her. She phoned the return number and Jeremy immediately answered.

"Julie, where are you? I would like to refer some of my patients, and I haven't seen you for a while."

She explained that the clinic was short of staff, so she had been reassigned there for the rest of the week. "Besides," she added, "at the end of this week my teaching rotation will be over. Another clinic nurse will be teaching the class for the next month, so she'll pick up your referrals." There was a brief silence, and Jeremy asked her for her home phone number. She obliged.

That same evening he phoned and invited her to attend the big football game between two local rival schools. She agreed, and planned for the outing that weekend. When they got to the game, there were no parking spots, but finally Jeremy found one in a residential area.

After the game, she thanked him for inviting her and returned home, exhausted from having walked so far to and from the car. He was scheduled to moonlight that evening, meaning he would be in the emergency room from 7:00 p.m. until the following morning.

The following week while she was working in the clinic, the hospital's overhead paging system announced her name. All of the nurses heard the page; it was a slow day, with few patients. The clinic nurses wondered who was paging her because she was not scheduled to conduct classes, but she refused to announce who it was. This time, Jeremy asked her to escort him to a party being given by the Chief of Staff that evening. It was such short notice that she first declined, only agreeing after he insisted. She regretted her decision, and later phoned him back to inform him she could not attend because she didn't feel well. In reality, she felt she wouldn't fit in being surrounded by physicians. Dr. Clark would not take no for an answer, though, and hopped in the car to drive to her house.

Julie looked out of her window and saw his car. She asked Margaret to tell him she was in bed, ill. Regardless, he asked if he could come in, so Margaret politely asked him to be seated on the sofa in the living room. This was the first time they had met, so they took the opportunity to become acquainted. They chatted for a while until Margaret suddenly remembered she had food on the stove, and asked to be excused to attend to her cooking. He stood up immediately to accompany her into the kitchen. He proceeded to lift the lid off a pot of dried beans Margaret was preparing for dinner, inhaling deeply and booming, "Oh, it smells wonderful!" Once he gained access in the kitchen, he felt he had gained Margaret's confidence, so he slipped into the hallway and knocked on Julie's door, not waiting for a response before he opened it. Julie was shocked at the impropriety of him seeing her lying in bed, but he barged in and insisted she get up and come to the party. She finally agreed to go with him, provided he return to the living room while she showered and dressed.

The Chief of Staff's house was in very upscale subdivision, at the end of a cul-de-sac surrounded by tall oak trees. A young boy with a guest list checked off the names as the entering guests identified themselves, giving each a nametag. When the two of them entered, the boy murmured, "Dr. and Mrs. Clark." Julie corrected him, but somehow it amused Dr. Clark.

The dinner party was quite formal, with waiters passing hors d'oeuvres, and vegetable trays placed throughout the house. Julie and Jeremy greeted many couples, and they found a breeze outside on the patio. As she stood with her hands folded, he took her picture, which he would later enlarge and keep for many years. The dinner was held in a large formal dining room that seated over fifty guests. Julie could hardly believe she was here, mingling with doctors she normally only assisted.

Afterwards, Julie returned to Dr. Clark's apartment to talk about the evening and the different people they met. He was quite interested to know her opinion. She explained at first she was reluctant to attend, but was glad she had changed her mind. She found the Chief of Staff soft- spoken and most considerate of others. Jeremy loved hearing her assessments of his colleagues, and decided the two of them would have a dinner party the following weekend. Julie smiled broadly; after the night they had just had, it sounded like fun.

First they had to plan a menu. After much discussion, they settled on roast beef, French green beans, squash soufflé, dinner rolls, red wine, unsweetened tea, and for dessert, apple pie à la mode. Julie had an amazing squash soufflé recipe that had been passed down through the family. She would prepare the vegetables, and he would prepare the meat. Jeremy asked her to prepare a grocery list and the two of them would go shopping the following weekend.

They went shopping at the grocery store near the college campus where Dr. Clark had attended medical school. She arrived at his house early that Saturday morning and they shopped for what seemed like hours. She was excited to show off her culinary skills, because she really enjoyed cooking. The guests were scheduled to arrive by six, so Julie decided she would prepare the vegetables at her house where her sister could help and advise her. Julie had to have everything prepared and packaged so she could return to Jeremy's apartment by four.

As she entered the apartment, she could smell the aroma of the beef roasted savored with onions, herbs, and garlic that had diffused throughout the apartment. She unpacked the vegetables and separated the serving dishes. She had brought her sister's best china and the electric knife. The meal would be served on a new teak table Dr. Clark had recently purchased. He had exquisite taste, and he introduced Julie to many things such as pewter, classical music, and various sports such as skiing, canoeing, football, and tennis. His favorite sport was ice hockey, which he had played since his childhood. In fact, he took her to see her first hockey game.

The doorbell rang; one of the three invited couples had arrived ahead of schedule. Jeremy invited them in and introduced them to her. She offered them a glass of wine before the meal was served and they graciously accepted. After the other two couples had arrived, and Julie and Jeremy began serving the meal after they were all seated. Everyone fell silent as they tasted the beautiful meal the hosts had so carefully planned and prepared. Moreover, the colorful arrangements made the décor of a fall festival for an hour of wholesome eating. The centerpiece made of freshly cut beautiful assorted flowers (Julie's sister's suggestion) made the table even more beautiful. The first comment was how good the squash soufflé was, although the guest had mistaken it for corn. Julie explained it was a squash casserole, and another guest explained she didn't like squash, but liked this enough to have a second serving!

After the guests left, Julie started to clean the kitchen, but Jeremy insisted she leave the dishes. He wanted to talk, like he always did after leaving a party, to get her opinion and to brag about what a hit the dinner was. Obviously he was proud how well the evening went. Julie, however, was accustomed to cleaning the kitchen; she had been raised not to leave any soiled utensils and dirty dishes for the morning. He became furious and went to the adjoining room and pouted, then returned to the kitchen and exclaimed, "I don't need a maid!"

Julie decided to leave. She was upset that he had gotten so angry, but after not hearing from him for days, she finally broke down and phoned him to ask if she could drop by to pick up her dishes and other items left from the dinner party. He promised to have them ready upon her arrival. She drove over to his apartment with trepidation in her heart; that night, he told her he planned to get married to his hometown sweetheart. Julie knew all along he had vowed to marry her, but for him to suddenly tell her was a bit surprising. She became a little teary-eyed for a moment, but after the hardships of the year before, this breakup was relatively mild.

Chapter XXIII

The Proposal/The Marriage

Julie adjusted quickly after the breakup with Jeremy; nothing could have been as devastating as the breakup with her first boyfriend. One of her co-workers introduced her to a young man who was an executive at a local bank. His name was Aaron and he was highly intelligent, having graduated among the top ten percent of his class at the University of Pittsburgh. His major was economics, with a minor in computer science. When they first met, she had just gotten off work, so she was wearing her nursing uniform; Aaron did not find her attractive. A year later they met again at a party; she was dressed in a nice hunter-green pants and a pink and green sweater that highlighted her cleavage, not to mention she was a perfect size eight. He couldn't keep his eyes off of her, but he did so in a subtle manner. After she had had enough dancing and started to leave, he asked her for her phone number. He phoned her the following week, and she invited him over. They talked about many things; he seemed to be knowledgeable on almost any subject matter. But she discovered he was not legally divorced, which concerned her. She decided to be unavailable each time he phoned her. He knew well he had no future with her until his divorce was finalized.

One Friday while she was at work, he phoned her and asked if she would join him downtown after work just for a few minutes because he had two things to share with her. She hesitated, but finally agreed. When she walked in the main entrance of the restaurant, someone from the bar called, "Hey, Julie." She saw that it was Aaron, surrounded by co-workers. He introduced her and asked if she wanted a glass of wine; before she could say no, he had ordered it. She wanted to know what he had to tell her, but he said it had to wait until they were alone.

His co-workers finally left, and Julie looked at him expectantly. Aaron smiled. It seemed he had been offered a job with an annual salary of $50,000 and his divorce was final; in fact, it had been made final months earlier, but he did not tell her because he did not think it was the appropriate time. She thought to herself, *Why is he telling me this and how do I fit into his plans?* but she continued to listen. It became clear when he told her, "The new job I took? It's in California. And I want your opinion on my plan to relocate."

Julie smiled; she was truly happy for him. "When do you have to move?" she asked.

"In the next two weeks," he replied. She nodded, and checked her watch; it was time to leave. He walked her to her car and promised to phone her the following day.

Chapter XXIV

The Move /California Dreaming

Two weeks passed and Aaron had moved. He phoned her almost daily, and they talked into the wee hours. He even phoned her while she was at work. One day as they were talking over the phone, one of the neighbors was visiting Margaret. Margaret told the neighbor the numerous times Julie's boyfriend would phone her and the hours they spent talking on the phone. The neighbor prophesized eventually he would marry her, and she would be moving. The neighbor was right because two months after Aaron had relocated, he proposed. But first they would have to live together to make sure they were right for each other. She turned in her resignation; the nurses gave her the biggest going-away party that she ever imagined.

That same evening she received a phone call from Dr. Clark. He claimed he just called to say hello, but Julie knew he'd heard the news that she was planning to marry and relocate. He asked if she would see him to say goodbye in person. She thought it couldn't possibly hurt because he was married, and she was going to get married, so she agreed to meet him at the plaza where they first met. He asked so many questions; if she loved him, what type of work he did, and where was he from. He wished her well, but conspicuously did not include her husband-to-be. Strangely, before departing, Jeremy asked Julie if she would have married him. She hesitated and eventually responded, "Yes, I would have married you."

He pressed her. " What about your family?

She smiled. "My family was not marrying you; I was.

Jeremy was silent. He couldn't stop embracing her until finally Julie insisted it was time to say farewell.

Aaron flew back to drive her to California. The drive was long and the weather was extremely hot, especially in El Paso, Texas. Aaron had an apartment in California that he shared with another co-worker; however, his co-worker was in the process of moving into a house. Julie couldn't understand how his co-worker, who had been on the same job for almost the same length of time as Aaron, was able to purchase a home.

Finally they were at least settled alone in their beautiful apartment. Unfortunately, it was difficult for her to adjust being away from home; she had lived all of her life in the south and only travelled outside of the state once. She figured she would just have to take time to get used to it.

Julie hoped to find a job at one of the three main hospitals, and she did get hired at the county hospital in an intensive care unit. The job required working at night, which was not the shift she wanted to work. After one month, she resigned and became employed at a Catholic hospital. The hospital was governed by nuns who worked on the floor with the regular staff. The patients were mostly indigents who couldn't afford to go to the doctor for regular check-ups, so they were very ill and required intensive care. Julie was miserable; she cried and complained to Aaron daily. Aaron would listen but reminded her of their goal: to buy a house. They were saving together, he always said.

Julie wasn't entirely convinced. She noticed during the evenings after dinner, Aaron wanted to sit and socialize with the neighbors at the swimming pool. Then she noticed he would buy wine and other alcohol that the neighbors desired. She confronted him about his spending habit more than once, which resulted in continual arguments. Yet he continued to socialize and to buy the neighbors refreshments until she decided it was time to withdraw all of the funds she deposited in their joint account. She did it the same day she resigned from her job.

Of course, it was not long before Aaron discovered what had happened. He asked her why she withdrew such a large sum of money from their account. She explained she felt the need to have her own savings account since he was supporting the community. Moreover, she secretly planned to have her car transported by a professional company … Aaron realized she was planning to leave him, so one Friday he came home from work early. Julie was surprised when he walked in and announced, "I don't want you to leave me. We are going to get married tonight." The little voice in her head told her not to marry him, but she felt sorry for him and she agreed. They flew to Lake Tahoe and became man and wife.

Aaron felt that he too had outgrown this small town and knew Julie hated living there, so the two of them moved to Los Angeles. She liked Los Angeles because she could go shopping at the upscale stores; the music on the radio was no longer country and western but jazz and R&B. She and Aaron moved into a beautiful townhouse where most of their neighbors were professionals such as physicians, lawyers, and teachers. Julie got a job at the Veterans Administration Hospital and, after a short time, became head nurse. She worked very hard to ensure her patients were taken care of according to her standards. The staff thought she was too strict, but they respected her because she never asked them to do anything she was not willing to do herself.

Julie would phone home daily to check on Margaret, who had begun to feel lonely. She began to spend the night with her friends and sometimes she would stay away from home for weeks. She would, however, phone Julie long distance to let her know where she was, but Julie felt she needed to come to California for a visit. So Margaret came to visit. She enjoyed being with Julie, but wanted to return home after a week.

Aaron's job at times would require him to remain overnight; at least that was what he told his Julie . At the end of a tumultuous week, Julie wanted to come home to talk to Aaron, but he was never home. On Fridays she would observe some of her neighbors barbecuing out on their patio and other families going out for dinner, but she was at home alone. Later she would find women's phone numbers in Aaron's shirt pockets and lipstick stains on his white collars. When she confronted him, he denied everything, accusing her of imagining things. One night she had a very profound revelation. William, who had been dead for nearly four years, came to her in a dream. He was seated in the lower level of a stadium and she was seated above him. In the dream, William looked up at her and said, "That man is not for you. He likes different women." She sat straight up in the bed; it was as though she had been in William's presence. Perhaps William's spirit was troubled that his little girl was being mistreated. Julie knew that there were decisions to be made, and those decisions would have to be made sooner rather than later.

Chapter XXV

The Breakup/The Divorce

Julie began daily to take inventory of her life. She was a loyal and dedicated nurse who worked tirelessly to ensure her patients received the highest standard of care. She took her marriage vows seriously as well; she wanted to make the marriage work. But there was one important factor she had to come to terms with: her spouse did not share those same values. He was free-spirited, a happy-go-lucky type of individual, whereas she was serious and aspired to have something in life.

Margaret would come each year to spend time with her, so she had an opportunity to observe the marriage over the years. One year when Margaret had come to visit, she said something that made Julie more determined than ever to file for a divorce. Margaret said, "I am afraid you two are going to be just like Aunt Elizabeth and Uncle Ray." Julie was quite disturbed, because Aunt Elizabeth and Uncle Ray were considered the black sheep of the family. They rented all of their lives and would get evicted every other month.

Once Margaret returned home, Julie continued to think about the statement her mother had made. She knew Aaron had been unfaithful and continued to remain so. So she began to do legal research on how to file for a no-fault divorce without legal representation, since there was no real property involved. She obtained the legal documents and signed her portion of the document. The evening she received and completed the documents, she handed Aaron the document for his signature. After he read it carefully, he tore it into shreds. Fortunately, she had a duplicate copy. This meant she would have to file the paper and incur a fee for placing an ad in the local paper. This also meant the divorce would not be final until six months later.

At last the final divorce papers arrived in the mail in a long brown envelope from the State of California. She opened the envelope and read the official document, entitled "Dissolution of Marriage," and the reason: "irreconcilable differences." She felt relieved that she was free to strive to achieve those things she felt she deserved. Prior to the divorce, anything she acquired was considered community property and Aaron would have been entitled to fifty percent. She read the paper over and over, she was so excited. After eight-and-a-half years of being mistreated, she was free of Aaron. She phoned him at work and congratulated him on becoming an official bachelor for the second time. He was quiet and asked her to explain. She informed him the divorce documents had arrived and he was free to leave.

Normally, Aaron never came home before 2:00 a.m., but this particular night, he returned home at 5: 00 p.m. He asked to see the document; he read it and tucked it away in his briefcase. He sat at the dining room table sipping a glass of wine until the entire bottle was emptied. He remained silent the entire night. He finally went to sleep on the sofa, where he would sleep until moving out.

The next day Julie went to work as she did each morning (she seldom would call out, even when she was ill). She didn't mention to anyone she was a single woman, but it seemed she didn't have to tell anyone because it was obvious she was happy; she had a noticeable glow. She was about to start a new life. Although she did not make a lot of money, she was determined to become a homeowner. Most of the single girls she knew had lived in California all of their lives and settled for living in an apartment. She met two elderly women in their seventies who never owned a home. She vowed that would never happen to her. She couldn't understand living in a city surrounded by so much wealth and not having part of the American dream.

Julie and Aaron went their separate ways. She made friends with her co-workers and became very close to her immediate supervisor who would later become like a sister. The supervisor was financially well-off, because she was frugal and her mother was wealthy. She lived in a very plush townhouse in the suburban area of Los Angeles near the Forum, former home of the Lakers. Anytime she decided she wanted an expensive piece of furniture, she would phone her mother and asked her to cash in one of her savings bonds, or she would ask for the interest earned on her savings accounts for that particular quarter. Julie was impressed that her supervisor's mother had acquired such wealth at a relatively young age. Julie knew she probably could not achieve that level of wealth, but she was still determined to become a homeowner, even in southern California.

Chapter XXVI

The Fulfilled Dream/The Miracles

One Sunday while Julie was returning from church, she drove down a beautiful street with many upscale condominiums. She saw a "For Sale" sign posted out front of one of the condominiums. She jotted down the telephone number and called when she got home. When a lady answered the phone, Julie explained she had been by earlier and asked if she could come by to take a look inside. The owner asked if she could come at 3:00 p.m. that day.

She drove with excitement but she was anxious because she knew this condo was well above her financial reach and perhaps she was being irrational. Her annual salary was only $28,000. Arriving at the condominium, Julie noticed the main entrance of the building was heavily secured; in order to gain access, visitors had to use the telephone stationed on a wall with a directory of the residents' last name and two numbers along side of their names. She picked up the phone and dialed the resident. As the phone was ringing, she happened to glance up and noticed there was a camera. The resident answered and Julie identified herself. The resident instructed her to open the door, turn right once she had entered the building, and proceed down the hallway

The corridor was very long, with carpet throughout. She reached unit 127 and rang the doorbell, and the door opened. A middle-aged woman with a British accent greeted her with a big smile and invited her inside. It was as though she had known her all of her life. Once she was inside the owner did not hesitate to point out the large sectional oak wooden floor in the foyer, which her husband had carefully chosen. She shared with Julie how ill he was; at that time, he remained in the hospital.

Left of the foyer was a small guest closet. Julie and the owner walked straight ahead to a relatively small but long kitchen, which the owner referred to as her favorite room because of the added amenities. Her husband had installed a microwave and a double self-cleaning oven. There was a double stainless-steel sink and the backdrop was a colorful brown and yellow tile that matched the countertop. The owner then guided Julie straight ahead into a separate dining room that had an elegant crystal chandelier. The view from the dining room window was simply breathtaking: evergreens, assorted flowers, shrubs, and many perennials, lit up at night as though it were Christmas all year round.

The owner remarked that the neighborhood was known for having residents who were luminaries. She pointed out that the condominium next door was where some of the Lakers lived during the off season. She also mentioned the twenty-four hour patrol.

The next area they toured was a large living room. There were no wooden floors but light beige plush carpet that extended from the dining room; Julie liked the romantic fireplace. To the right of the living room was a small study with wall-to-wall bookshelves. The living room had two sliding doors that led outside onto the patio, on which sat beautiful heavy white lawn furniture

Returning inside, the owner led Julie to the master bedroom and a huge walk-in closet, and master bathroom with a separate shower and a Jacuzzi tub. That was the end of the tour. Julie's heart began to accelerate, because now she needed to know the asking price. The owner explained she should ask for $100,000 but she would reduce her price for Julie to $85,000. Julie remembered how her sister had entered many counteroffers during the times when she purchased her second home, and she had taken a second mortgage. Julie asked the owner if she would consider accepting an offer with two mortgages. The owner thought before saying she would have to discuss it with her husband when she visited him at the hospital later that evening. She promised to get back to Julie that night.

Julie was filled with excitement after having been shown the most beautiful condominium she had ever laid eyes on, yet she felt anxious. Since she was newly divorced and had incurred expenses as head of the household, she only had $1,000 in her savings account at the moment. She began to think of ways to earn money quickly to enhance her savings for the down payment. One sure way was to work overtime at the hospital, because there was always a need. Suddenly she asked herself, *What if the seller won't accept a second mortgage, and what if the bank declines my loan? After all, there was an unpaid bill I signed with Aaron once.* All sorts of questions surfaced. She arrived home and began to clean all three rooms thoroughly. She always found cleaning to be therapeutic, especially when she was stressed or contemplating making difficult decisions. She worked so hard that she fell asleep on the sofa. The phone rang which awakened her.

She picked up the phone and a voice said, "Hello, Julie." She hesitated to in an attempt to determine the caller's identity. The caller continued, "This is Ms. Morris, the owner of the condominium. I discussed your offer with my husband and we both have agreed to accept taking a second mortgage in the amount of $17,500, which would make the monthly note $165." Ms. Morris proceeded to explain that her new townhome was under construction and would not be ready for another three months; they could close escrow at that time.

Julie was thrilled; she believed it had to be God's blessing, because she would have time to save one of her paychecks. She accepted the terms but realized she had to sign papers to present to the bank. She worked overtime and every other paycheck was deposited in her savings account. After two months, Julie had a total of $8,000 deposited into her savings.

Thirty days before closing, she went to a local savings and loan. She was so nervous that she could hardly speak. The bank had a crowd waiting in line to speak with the loan officer. She got in line and shortly afterwards, a young woman came out of a nearby office and reminded those who were waiting that they needed to sign in. Finally about an hour, Julie went in to speak with the loan officer. The officer was a small Hispanic man who wore glasses. She did not waste any time in explaining she was interested in purchasing a condominium and was requesting the bank to finance $76,000. The loan officer listened intently. He explained she would have to submit an application, and asked her how much money she planned to put towards the loan. She informed the loan officer she was prepared to put $8,000 down, and would provide $2000 as good faith. The loan officer seemed pleased but cautioned her final loan approval would take about ten business days and was contingent upon her credit score. She completed the application along with a check in the amount of $2,000. She left the bank hopeful the bank would approve the loan.

Approximately one week after completing a bank loan application, she received a letter from the bank. The letter had one line that asked Julie for a statement explaining the reason she was delayed in paying a previous loan—the same loan she had co-signed with Aaron. She sat down and carefully wrote a letter explaining she had co-signed with her ex-husband, and subsequently paid the loan because of his failure to do so. Three days later, she received a phone call from the bank informing her loan was approved and she needed to return to the bank to sign documents in order to finalize the loan. She jumped up and down and the first person she phoned was Margaret to tell her the great news.

Julie and the seller met at an escrow company in a city south of Los Angeles where the terms of the second mortgage loan were outlined such as the date of the month each payment was due and the penalty imposed if the payment was delinquent, and the fact the total loan would come due in five years. She didn't know this was considered a balloon payment. But she had faith in God she would be able to pay the $17,500 within five years. The first mortgage payment was $847 a month and $160 for the second mortgage, plus the $110 monthly association dues. There would hardly be any money left. She phoned Margaret and told her she was closing and had very little money left to go back and forth to work and to buy food. She never asked Margaret for anything, but was just talking casually. Margaret was not wealthy but was rich in spirit and would go above and beyond to help her children, especially Julie. At the end of the conversation, Margaret told her to be sweet and she would be hearing from her very soon.

On January 8, 1985, Julie moved into her new condominium. She was so elated that her dream was fulfilled. She did not have extra money to spend, but she was more contented than she had ever been in her life. Two weeks after she moved into the condominium; she received a check in the mail for a total of $250 as a refund from her previous phone carrier. Additionally, she received $300 deposit back from her previous landlord. Moreover, within the same two weeks Margaret sent her all except twenty dollars of her monthly entitlement check. She opened the letter and saw that Margaret had purchased a United States Postal Money Order for $500, payable to Julie. She went immediately to the local post office to cash it. The postal worker asked for identification, and afterwards counted the money at least three times. Julie also counted with the postal worker. Yet, when Julie returned home, she recounted the money and discovered she had a total of $550. She had been taught the importance of being honest and forthright, so she decided to go back to the post office to report the worker had given her more money back than she should have. The postal employee's supervisor was notified, and the supervisor explained she would notify Julie if there had been an error. Julie provided her full name and telephone number. The next day she received a message to phone the post office. Upon returning the phone call, the supervisor explained that there was no error found the previous day!

Julie would go on to resign from the Veterans Hospital to work at a company that was located in North Hollywood; within six months, she was promoted to supervisor with a new salary more than sufficient to meet her monthly obligations. Still, she constantly worried about having a note that was due in full within five years. After residing in the condominium for three years, she began to think of ways to repay the second mortgage. She went to another bank and applied for a loan to refinance both the first and the second mortgage. As a result of refinancing, she received $3,000 that she immediately deposited into her savings account.

She realized Margaret was lonely and was getting older, so she asked her to come live with her in California. They were more like roommates than mother and daughter. Margaret enjoyed the beautiful weather and the many cookouts. After two years, she wanted to return home; however, she did not want to return unless Julie moved back with her. Julie tried to explain she had a mortgage to pay and couldn't just leave. She saw the dilemma Margaret was facing—wanting to stay with her daughter but at the same time longing to return home. So she decided to rent the condominium out and return home. She advertised in the local paper and in less than a week an aspiring actor signed a rental agreement. The bank where he would deposit the monthly rent was nationally and internationally established, which enabled Julie to monitor each time he paid the rent.

Seven years later, she would sell the condominium. Looking back, she was happy with her decision to move back home with Margaret. She thought often of the fun times the two of them had living in sunny California, especially the many weekend trips to Las Vegas, and attending church each Sunday morning. But she was most proud of her decision to honor Margaret's request to return home and to have the many family gatherings at the homestead with her children and grandchildren. Perhaps Margaret felt the need to be with the entire family, because she died ten years later of cancer.

Julie met a young man five years prior to Margaret's death; he would become her lifetime friend. Margaret was fond of him, and he had a deep love for her. It is comforting to know that Margaret did have an opportunity to meet this individual, and approved of him. Today there is a bond between him and Julie that will remain until perpetuity.

Epilogue

Before we are born, our lives are destined by our Creator. We are charged to search deep into our inner souls to seek the real meaning and purpose of our existence. If we fail to seek our purpose, will, and plan, we will spend a lifetime missing the happiness, contentment, unspeakable joy, and full richness that no material possession can ever bring to rest within our souls. We should tune in constantly to our Creator to seek His will, because when we come to the end of this life, we do not want to have any regrets. It is in that hour we suddenly become aware of the value and true meaning of living a wholesome and rewarding life, versus having been caught up in life's daily struggle, striving to meet the expectations set by a misguided society. Without having lived according to the will and purpose of our Creator, our lives are futile. Perhaps Julie's view of herself is much like that of the unknown author's:

> I have to live with myself, and so I want to be fit for myself, to know always to look myself straight in the eye. I don't want to stand with the setting sun, and hate myself for the things I have done. I don't want to keep me on a closet shelf and fool myself as I come and go into thinking that nobody else will know the

kind of person I really am—I don't want to dress myself up in sham. I want to go out with my head erect; I want to deserve all man's respect; and here in the struggle for fame and wealth, I want to be able to like myself. I don't want to look at myself and know that I am a bluffer, an empty show. I can never hide myself from me; I see what others may never see. I know what others may never know; I never can fool myself and so, whatever happens, I want to be self-respecting and guilt-free.

Unknown Author

LaVergne, TN USA
10 March 2010
175570LV00004B/41/P

9 781449 042295